JAZZ PLAY-ALONG

Book and Audio for B♭, E♭, C and Bass Clef Instruments

Volume 184

Arranged and Produced by Mark Taylor

Speed • Pitch • Balance • Loop

Jimmy SMITH

T0039928

TITLE	PAGE NUMBERS			
	C Treble Instruments	B♭ Instruments	E♭ Instruments	C Bass Instruments
Back at the Chicken Shack	4	18	30	44
The Cat	5	19	31	45
Dot Com Blues	6	20	32	46
Gracie	8	22	34	48
Hobo Flats	9	23	35	49
Judo Mambo	10	24	36	50
Midnight Special	12	26	38	52
Organ Grinders Swing	13	27	39	53
The Sermon	16	17	42	43
Walk on the Wild Side	14	28	40	54

To access audio visit:
www.halleonard.com/mylibrary

Enter Code
5548-1193-2394-0867

Cover photo © Paul Hoeffler/CTSIMAGES

ISBN 978-1-4803-8731-7

7777 W. BLUEMOUND RD. P.O. BOX 13819 MILWAUKEE, WI 53213

Visit Hal Leonard Online at
www.halleonard.com

JIMMY SMITH

Volume 184

Arranged and Produced
by Mark Taylor

Featured Players:

Graham Breedlove–Trumpet/Flugelhorn
John Desalme–Saxes
Tony Nalker–Keyboards
Jim Roberts–Guitar
Paul Henry–Bass
Todd Harrison–Drums

Recorded at Bias Studios, Springfield, Virginia
Bob Dawson, Engineer

HOW TO USE THE AUDIO:

Each song has <u>two</u> tracks:

1) Split Track/Melody

Woodwind, Brass, Keyboard, and **Mallet Players** can use this track as a learning tool for melody style and inflection.

Bass Players can learn and perform with this track – remove the recorded bass track by turning down the volume on the LEFT channel.

Keyboard and **Guitar Players** can learn and perform with this track – remove the recorded piano part by turning down the volume on the RIGHT channel.

2) Full Stereo Track

Soloists or **Groups** can learn and perform with this accompaniment track with the RHYTHM SECTION only.

BACK AT THE CHICKEN SHACK

BY JIMMY SMITH

C VERSION

THE CAT

C VERSION

BY LALO SCHIFRIN

DOT COM BLUES

GRACIE

BY JIMMY SMITH

C VERSION

HOBO FLATS

C VERSION

BY OLIVER NELSON

JUDO MAMBO

BY JIMMY SMITH

C VERSION

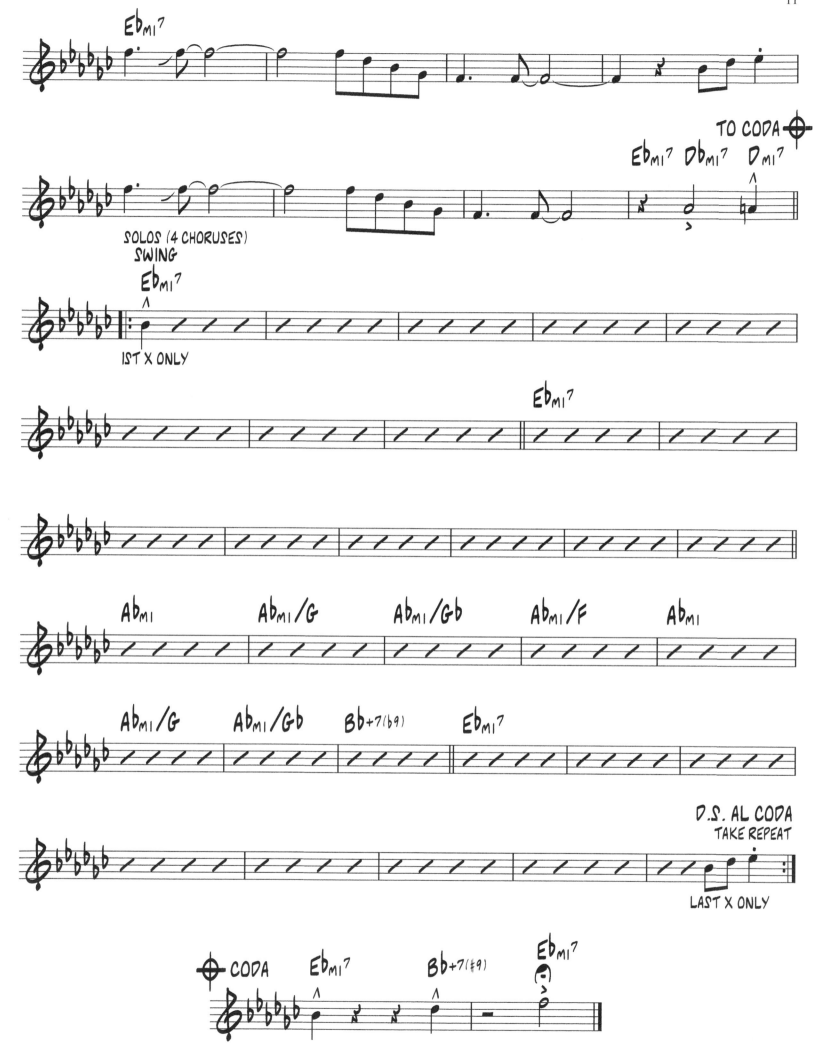

MIDNIGHT SPECIAL

BY JIMMY SMITH

Organ Grinders Swing

Words by Irving Mills and Mitchell Parish
Music by Will Hudson

C Version

WALK ON THE WILD SIDE

LYRIC BY MACK DAVID
MUSIC BY ELMER BERNSTEIN

C VERSION

THE SERMON

BY HAMPTON HAWES

C VERSION

THE SERMON

BY HAMPTON HAWES

Bb VERSION

BACK AT THE CHICKEN SHACK

BY JIMMY SMITH

Bb VERSION

THE CAT

Bb VERSION

BY LALO SCHIFRIN

Dot Com Blues

By Jimmy Smith

Bb Version

GRACIE

By Jimmy Smith

HOBO FLATS

BY OLIVER NELSON

Judo Mambo

BY JIMMY SMITH

Bb VERSION

MIDNIGHT SPECIAL

BY JIMMY SMITH

Bb VERSION

Organ Grinders Swing

Words by Irving Mills and Mitchell Parish
Music by Will Hudson

WALK ON THE WILD SIDE

LYRIC BY MACK DAVID
MUSIC BY ELMER BERNSTEIN

Bb VERSION

Back at the Chicken Shack

BY JIMMY SMITH

THE CAT

Eb VERSION

BY LALO SCHIFRIN

DOT COM BLUES

Eb Version

BY JIMMY SMITH

GRACIE

Eb Version

BY Jimmy Smith

Hobo Flats

BY OLIVER NELSON

Judo Mambo

BY JIMMY SMITH

Eb Version

MIDNIGHT SPECIAL

BY JIMMY SMITH

Eb VERSION

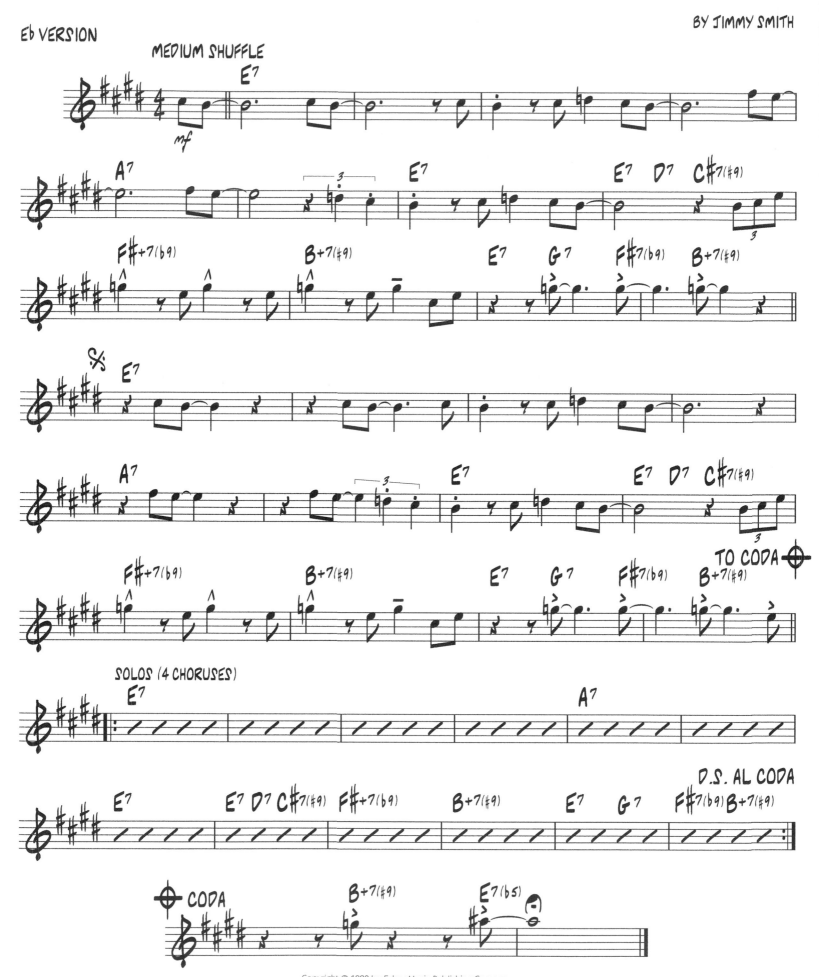

Organ Grinders Swing

Eb Version

Words by Irving Mills and Mitchell Parish
Music by Will Hudson

WALK ON THE WILD SIDE

LYRIC BY MACK DAVID
MUSIC BY ELMER BERNSTEIN

Eb VERSION

SOLOS (3 CHORUSES)

ORGAN & GUITAR _____

RIT.

BASS _____

THE SERMON

BY HAMPTON HAWES

Eb VERSION

THE SERMON

BY HAMPTON HAWES

BACK AT THE CHICKEN SHACK

By Jimmy Smith

THE CAT

BY LALO SCHIFRIN

DOT COM BLUES

BY JIMMY SMITH

GRACIE

BY JIMMY SMITH

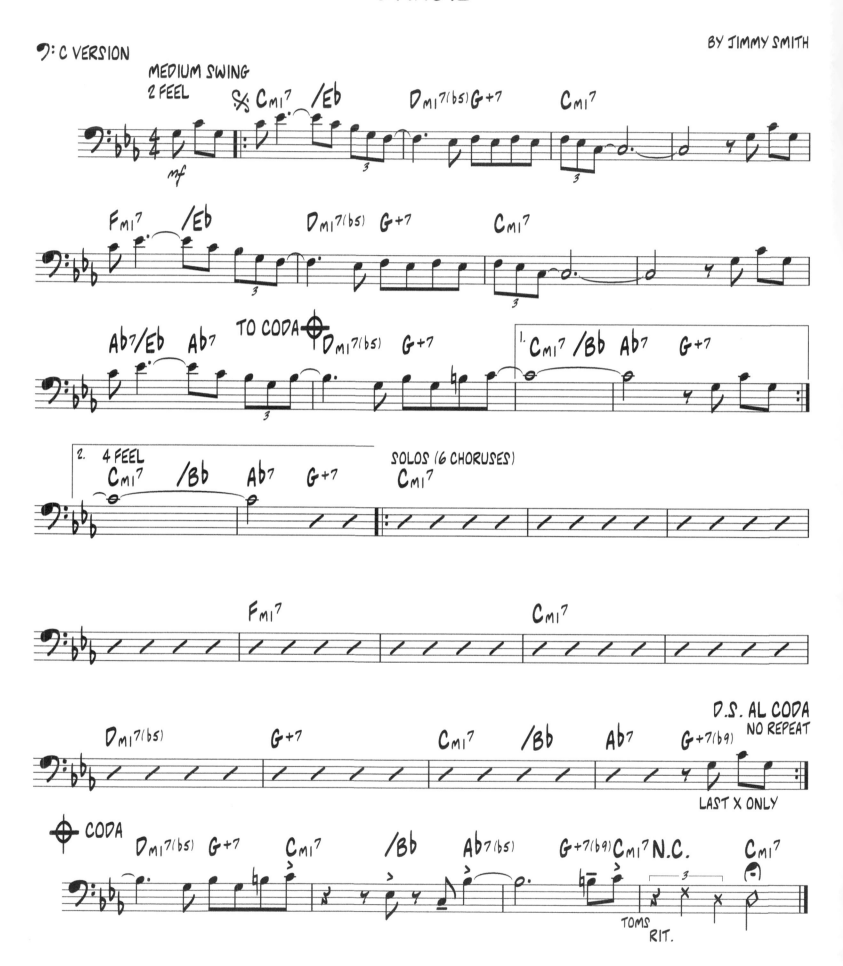

HOBO FLATS

BY OLIVER NELSON

JUDO MAMBO

BY JIMMY SMITH

C VERSION

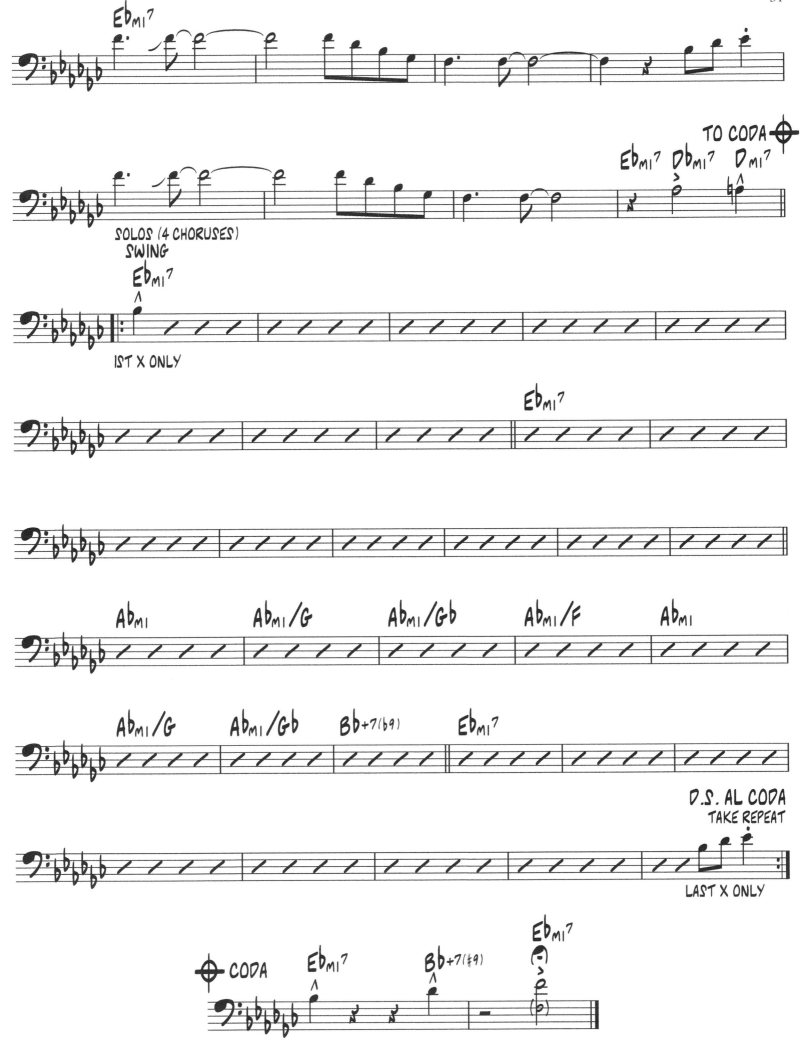

MIDNIGHT SPECIAL

BY Jimmy Smith

Organ Grinders Swing

WORDS BY IRVING MILLS AND MITCHELL PARISH
MUSIC BY WILL HUDSON

WALK ON THE WILD SIDE

LYRIC BY MACK DAVID
MUSIC BY ELMER BERNSTEIN

Presenting the Hal Leonard JAZZ PLAY-ALONG® SERIES

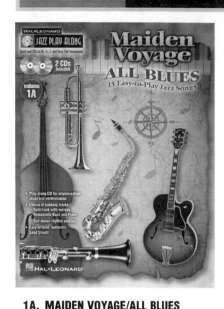

For use with all B-flat, E-flat, Bass Clef and C instruments, the Jazz Play-Along® Series is the ultimate learning tool for all jazz musicians. With musician-friendly lead sheets, melody cues, and other split-track audio choices included, these first-of-a-kind packages help you master improvisation while playing some of the greatest tunes of all time. FOR STUDY, each tune includes a split track with: melody cue with proper style and inflection • professional rhythm tracks • choruses for soloing • removable bass part • removable piano part. FOR PERFORMANCE, each tune also has: an additional full stereo accompaniment track (no melody) • additional choruses for soloing.